this journal
belongs to

....

Jesus, You're All I Need

DEVOTIONAL JOURNAL FOR GIRLS

BELLE CITY GIFTS

Belle City Gifts
Racine, Wisconsin, USA

Belle City Gifts is an imprint of BroadStreet Publishing Group LLC.
Broadstreetpublishing.com

Jesus, You're All I Need — a devotional journal for girls

ISBN 978-1-4245-5060-9

Devotional entries composed by AmyJo Benson, Cari Dugan, and Cate Mezyk.

Design by Chris Garborg | www.garborgdesign.com
Editorial services by Michelle Winger | www.literallyprecise.com

Printed in China.

17 18 19 20 21   7 6 5 4 3 2

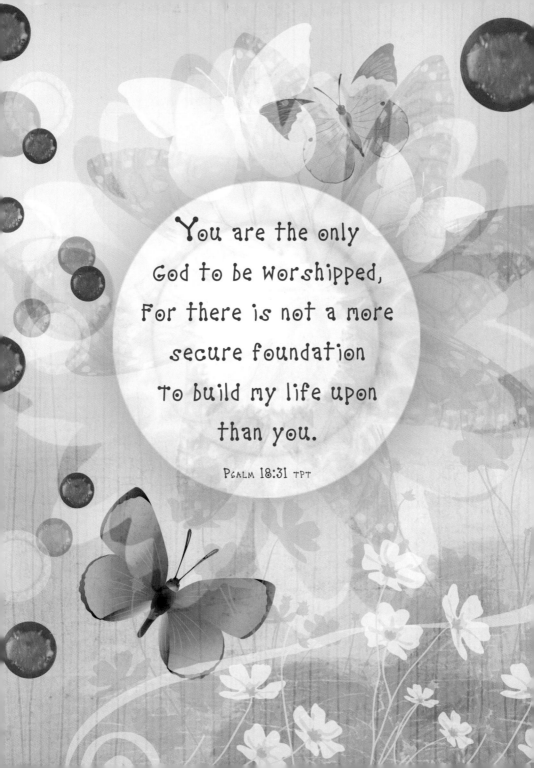

You are the only
God to be worshipped,
For there is not a more
secure foundation
to build my life upon
than you.

PSALM 18:31 TPT

Introduction

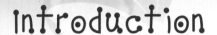

This devotional journal is written for girls
of all ages—just like you! It will engage
you in topics specific to the issues you
face each day. Read about themes like
beauty, courage, dignity, identity, integrity,
and value, and be encouraged to find
everything you need in Christ! Gain
confidence as you learn that the God who
created you delights in spending time
with you. Write down your thoughts in the
journaling space provided as you embrace
these words of truth.

ACCEPTANCE

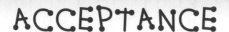

"Those the Father has given me will come to me,
and I will never reject them."
JOHN 6:37 NLT

We all long to feel part of a community or group because we were created to be in close relationships with each other. The Lord knit in us the desire for friendships that are close and life giving.

But sometimes we can feel left out from a group and we ache to belong. It can be very painful to feel unappreciated and unwelcome. Feeling unloved is a lonely place to be. Sometimes we go to great lengths in order to feel acceptance from our peers. We may do little things like change hairstyles or try to fit in by what we wear. We might even betray our morals and values in order to fit in and feel accepted.

God wants you to know that you are perfect the way you are. You do not need to change the way you look, or who you are to feel his acceptance. He knows you completely and loves you deeply. That ache you feel to belong? Go to him, let him fill it with the knowledge that you already do belong. You belong to him. His arms are open and ready to embrace you—just as you are.

What about yourself do you feel like you need to change in order to be accepted by others? List it here and ask God to give you an idea of what he thinks of you.

ADORATION

"You are a people holy to the Lᴏʀᴅ your God. The Lᴏʀᴅ your God has chosen you to be a people for his treasured possession, out of all the peoples who are on the face of the earth."

Deuteronomy 7:6 ᴇꜱᴠ

You are like a precious flower. You are absolutely the apple of your Father's eye. He loves and cherishes you beyond comprehension. Daughter, you are *adored*.

When you adore something, you don't just love it; you watch it, protect it, and handle it with great care. Your Father doesn't want to miss a thing. He wants to know every detail of your life. He handles you with such great care because he wants you to fully become who he intended you to be.

Because God adores us, he allows us to go through some things that don't always feel good. But God is perfect. He is good, loving, and protective. We can trust that in those difficult moments, he is shaping and molding us to be more like him—to grow fully into who he wants us to be.

What are some ways you feel God adores you? Can you see how you have become a richer person through some of the difficulties he has allowed to cross your path? Do you recognize his goodness even in those times?

He forgives me everytime I mess up
I feel more loved.
I know he will never give up on me

ANGER

"Don't sin by letting anger control you."
Don't let the sun go down while you are still angry.
EPHESIANS 4:26 NLT

There are many things in this world that make us angry, that *should* make us angry. Sometimes all it takes is turning on the five o'clock news and being confronted with injustice and hardship; it causes our blood to boil. Even though anger sounds bad, anger in itself is not wrong. God created us to feel deeply in a wide range of emotions. It is the way we respond in our anger that could be potentially fatal. If we allow our anger to get the best of us, it could destroy relationships or cause heartache and deep pain.

In our anger we always have a choice. We could lash out and be destructive, or we could allow our anger to evoke change in an unjust situation. It is possible to feel angry, yet exercise restraint and self-control when encountering unpleasant or unfair circumstances.

We can take comfort that God knows how we are feeling in every moment—in every situation—and that he cares deeply. He will help us choose to be loving and grace-giving if we feel as if our anger is spiraling out of control. All we have to do is ask him. He will not abandon us in our emotions.

Think back to the last time you were angry.
How do you feel that your anger controlled you,
or that you controlled your anger?

ANXIETY

Cast all your anxiety on him because he cares for you.
1 PETER 5:7 NIV

Your stomach feels like it's doing flips, your mind is stuck on repeat, everything feels more intense than usual, and sleep doesn't come easy. These are all signs of anxiety. Anxiety can be difficult to deal with, and sometimes it can begin taking over the way you do life.

If you ever find yourself in this state, immediately go to God. He does not want you to struggle with anxiety. When he sees you with so much mental and emotional weight, he wants to give you rest. He can take all of your anxiety and replace it with peace.

Tell God all the things that are overwhelming you. Go through each thing and picture yourself giving it to him. Ask him to help you stop the thoughts that play over and over in your head. Ask for *peace*. Your Heavenly Father loves you and he wants to comfort you. When unhealthy levels of anxiety arise, go to the Lord and allow him to lift you up. He will carry you through the situation and give you peace.

Are you struggling with anxiety? What things are causing you to be anxious? Take some time to give those things to the Lord and ask him to bring you comfort and peace.

AUTHENTICITY

"God sees not as man sees, for man looks at the outward appearance, but the Lord looks at the heart."
1 Samuel 16:7 NASB

Honest and genuine relationships are priceless. When we hide who we are, it becomes almost impossible for those who love us to enter into our lives and truly know us. A shallow friendship is empty and lonely. In order to have solid friendships, we need to let our guards down and let others into the hidden areas in our lives.

It can be scary to be open and transparent, but by doing so we are able to create true relationships that encourage and strengthen us in our weakest areas. Living an authentic life allows us to see that we aren't alone in our struggles. Each of us has our ups and our downs. We need each other.

There is much joy and freedom to be found in being who you are. This includes your relationship with God. Sometimes we forget that he already knows the inner workings of our hearts. Even though we may try, it is impossible to hide our struggles and shortcomings from him. Yet, he still loves us despite our faults and embraces us even more. He should be our standard for all other relationships.

Are you the same *you* when you are alone as you are when you are with other people? Do you struggle to show your true beautiful colors to those around you? What do you think will happen if you let others in? Let God show you today how much he loves you just for who you are!

BEAUTY

Don't be concerned about the outward beauty of fancy hairstyles, expensive jewelry, or beautiful clothes. You should clothe yourselves instead with the beauty that comes from within, the unfading beauty of a gentle and quiet spirit, which is so precious to God.
1 Peter 3:3-4 NLT

God's definition of beauty can become clouded in the face of the world's description. You can't open up a magazine or social media window and not be bombarded with images of pretty women: photoshopped and scantily-clothed.

The danger of these images is that we try to compare ourselves with them. We size up our appearance and feel ugly in comparison. Thoughts like, *I am not skinny enough to be beautiful,* or *My nose is too big to be beautiful* begin to worm themselves into the core of our beings. We begin to claim ownership to these lies instead of embracing the truth that God wants us to know and live by.

We are beautiful. From the top of our heads to the bottom of our toes. Knowing we are truly beautiful begins with us absorbing what the Lord thinks of us. Not only are we outwardly beautiful in our Creator's eyes, but inwardly too.

We all possess a beauty that it not easily seen on billboards or on TV. We harbor a beauty that surpasses any worldly definition. Our grace. Our patience . Our compassion. Our generosity. Our kindness. All of these things make us beautiful in God's eyes.

What do you see when you look in the mirror? Do you truly know and believe that you are beautiful on the inside and out?

BOLDNESS

I remind you to fan into flame the gift of God... for God gave us a spirit not of fear but of power and love and self-control.
2 Timothy 1:6-7 ESV

Any new situation can be daunting. A new school. A new job. A new group of friends. A new adventure or opportunity. All of these things can cause our knees to buckle and our heart to race.

Sometimes we need boldness for the concrete and tangible fears we face; an angry family member, a disgruntled friend, a failed test. Or maybe we need boldness to defend the weak and rise up for the forgotten. Sometimes we simply need boldness to do what we know is right.

Many times, we just want to cower and hide, but hiding doesn't make fears disappear. Instead, they are allowed to fester and grow. Before we know it, fear is taking control of our lives.

You may wish that you were braver. You *can* be. God has equipped you with everything you need to conquer any situation. He has given you the weapons to fight with—chin up and shoulders squared. You never have to go into any situation afraid. You can have full assurance that God will give you the boldness you need in the exact moment you need it.

God made you a warrior. Warriors don't run from scary situations; they march forward and battle on.

What situations can you think of that require you to be bold? Ask God to show you just how brave you can be when you depend on him.

COMFORT

You have given me many troubles and bad times,
but you will give me life again.
When I am almost dead,
you will keep me alive.
You will make me greater than ever,
and you will comfort me again.

PSALM 71:20-21 NCV

As Christians, we are never promised that we will go through life seeing no trouble. In fact, it's quite the opposite. We're told time and time again in the Bible that there will be tough times, that we will be persecuted for our beliefs, and we won't always have a life of ease.

But there is good news despite all that. We have someone we can always turn to in our times of pain. God is waiting for us to run to him. He is the greatest comforter we could ever find. He wants to restore us, refresh us, and bring us contentment amidst the darkness of our anguish.

You can always turn to Jesus during times of trial. He will open his arms and welcome you, helping you find your way through it all. If you feel burdened by what life has offered you, pray for his peace today. He will restore you over and over again.

In what areas do you need God's comfort today?
Tell him about it. He is listening.

COMMITMENT

I know that you delight to set your truth deep in my spirit.
So come into the hidden places of my heart
And teach me wisdom.

PSALM 51:6 TPT

Commitment, follow-through, and *faithfulness* are all words that mean about the same thing. They are character traits that God desires in you. Some things we commit to because they seem fun or easy. Other things deserve our commitment because they are the right things to do. These are the commitments that are often more difficult to stick with.

Faithfulness is one of the nine fruits of the spirit written in Galatians 5:22-23. It holds great value before God. As his daughter, you are an example and a light to many. When God calls you to be faithful, it means that you do what you say you are going to do even when it is inconvenient. You stick with it because others are depending on you.

By learning to be a more faithful person, you will find that others trust and respect you deeply. Jesus was faithful to his Father in the most difficult commitment imaginable—being crucified on the cross for our sins. Because of Jesus' faithfulness to his commitment, we are able to be in relationship with the Father. *That* is something to be extremely grateful for.

How can you show faithfulness in areas you have committed yourself to? Do you see the value of being faithful in those areas? Thank the Lord for his commitment to you today.

CONFIDENCE

The Lᴏʀᴅ will be your confidence
and will keep your foot from being caught.
Pʀᴏᴠᴇʀʙs 3:26 ᴇsᴠ

It is so amazing to think there is only one *you* in this entire world! Only one with your laugh, your face, your quirks, and your specific talents. No other person can be you better than you. God made you with great intention—every inch of you inside and out—and he doesn't make mistakes.

You are beautiful in God's eyes, and he created you for a purpose. The only way you can fully accomplish his purpose for your life is to get to know yourself and accept the beautiful person you are. When you do this, you wear an outfit called *confidence*. It's the kind of clothing that shines bright and attracts others to its light.

Seek the Lord and he will reveal more of who you were created to be. You may see talents come forth that you never knew you had. There is a mission for you in life: love and accept yourself for who you are. Be you; nobody can do it better!

What are some talents you feel God has given you? Are there areas in which you feel insecure? Pray for the Lord to bring you full confidence in who you are.

CONTENTMENT

I know how to live on almost nothing or with everything. I have learned the secret of living in every situation, whether it is with a full stomach or empty, with plenty or little. For I can do everything through Christ, who gives me strength.

PHILIPPIANS 4:12-13 NLT

Have you ever looked at someone else's life and wistfully thought, *I wish I had what they had?*

It seems harmless enough, but when those thoughts grow and multiply (as they are known to do), they become dangerous. When we allow discontentment to foster in our lives, we are really allowing our joy to be taken from us. Discontentment gives our hearts permission to wander in directions that are not good. Our priorities are in danger of becoming hazy.

When discontentment takes root in our lives, we may find that it is affecting the relationships around us. Instead of partaking in a friend's joy over their successes and accomplishments, we begin to envy and resent them. There are no winners in a comparison game. We become so focused on what we want or don't have that it becomes impossible to notice and be thankful for what we are blessed with. Discontentment makes us unhappy and miserable .It inhibits us from enjoying and embracing every moment of life.

Sometimes the only way to battle discontentment is to continually number your blessings, and thank God for his goodness. It's a practical way to keep discontentment at bay. What things in life are you thankful for?

COURAGE

"So do not fear, for I am with you; do not be dismayed, for I am your God. I will strengthen you and help you; I will uphold you with my righteous right hand."

Isaiah 41:10 NIV

The Bible is chock full of courageous girls. Esther faced possible death or severe punishment from her husband the king just for asking him to dinner. Ruth followed her mother-in-law to a new country where life was full of unknowns because she felt it was the right thing to do. Hannah gave up her son because she knew he belonged in the house of the Lord. Noah's wife got on a boat when there wasn't a drop of water to be found anywhere and everyone thought she was crazy. She obeyed God's command alongside her family.

In your lifetime, you will come upon many situations where you will need to muster up your courage. Whether it's standing up to your friends for what's right, taking a leap into the unknown, or making a change in your life, you can do it if you take hold of the Lord's hand and ask for his strength.

God is willing to walk you through anything if you'll ask him to. Do you need courage today? Ask for his help and he will give you strength.

CREATIVITY

We are what he has made us, created in Christ Jesus for good works, which God prepared beforehand to be our way of life.
Ephesians 2:10 NRSV

Everyone has a creative streak. God made us to create in various mediums. We could be defined as writers, musicians, painters, builders, athletes, dancers, chefs, photographers...the list is endless. Have you ever created something and then stepped back to admire it? You might have even been awe-struck, filled with pride and admiration over what you had created. Artists go to great lengths to make sure their work is not only seen, but also preserved.

This is how God looks at you. You are his greatest work of art, created for a wonderful purpose. He doesn't focus on your flaws; he sees his perfect creation, and he thinks it is wonderful. He thinks *you* are wonderful.

Sometimes you might feel like you aren't worthy. You may look at yourself with disgust and disdain, wishing you had a different gift, talent, or personality. And it breaks God's heart. If only you could see yourself the way God sees you. You would be completely blown away if you knew just how much he admires you. You are not a mistake. Your hair color, your smile, your interests, your abilities, they were all orchestrated by the Creator. No piece of artwork is the same. No piece can be duplicated. Each is unique and special to the artist.

How do you look at yourself? As a masterpiece or as a flawed piece of art? The second one does not exist in God's eyes. Ask him to show you just how wonderful he thinks you are.

DELIGHT

"The LORD your God in your midst,
The Mighty One, Will save;
He Will rejoice over you With gladness,
He Will quiet you With His love,
He Will rejoice over you With singing."

ZEPHANIAH 3:17 NKJV

Did you know that the mighty God, Creator of heaven and earth, is a proud Papa? That's right! He is a loving Father who delights in you—his daughter! He created you not just so you can enjoy him, but also that he may enjoy you.

Every good thing that is in this world is from God and teaches us about his character. Humor and laughter are a part of who he is. Art and creativity are a part of who he is. Peace and quiet, along with excitement and surprises, are all a part of who he is. There are many things that he enjoys, but we are at the top of his list.

God delights in the way you see things, the sweet thoughts you have, the things that make you laugh, and the way you represent him. He delights in your hard work and what makes you determined in life. He delights in you because he made you. He is not looking for perfection; he just wants a relationship.

Like a parent delights in their child, so your heavenly Father delights in you. You are his. He loves you, and nothing can change that. List some things about you that you feel God delights in.

DIGNITY

She is clothed with strength and dignity;
she can laugh at the days to come.
PROVERBS 31:25 NIV

When Proverbs 31 describes the perfect woman, one of the key ways she is described is as being *dignified*. What exactly does it mean to be dignified? It means having pride in who you are, and it's a quality that commands respect.

Would people looking at your life from the outside see dignity? Would they describe you as being worthy of respect? Are your actions and decisions speaking as one who takes pride in who they are?

God calls us to clothe ourselves in dignity, or to wrap ourselves up in it so completely that we become the very essence of the word.

Take a look at your life and your day-to-day actions. Do you believe that the way you are presenting yourself to the world is respectful? As you get dressed, envision yourself first putting on dignity. Wrap yourself up in it. Pray that the Lord will help you in this endeavor, clothing you in decorum, grace, and honor.

Think of a woman you would describe as having dignity. What makes you think of her that way? How can you make dignity a part of your being as well?

DILIGENCE

The plans of the diligent lead to profit
as surely as haste leads to poverty.
PROVERBS 21:5 NIV

Success is hard to measure. Who is successful? The one who tries her very best and gives it her all? Or the one who puts forth just enough effort to get the job done? Do you ever wonder why you should do things with all of your heart? Why you should finish every single project or assignment well? Why you should even bother?

Perhaps the project at hand is insignificant or unimportant. It could very well be possible that no one will ever see or acknowledge your efforts. It could be a tedious and unpleasant task—one that might not seem worth your time or attention. There is much value in diligently putting your all into it anyway.

Nothing good comes out of not trying our best. There's no success or sense of pride and accomplishment. There is no reward in cutting corners. Who wants to be known for their lack of attention to detail, their careless ways, or lazy, half-hearted attempts?

Being diligent every day takes a lot of effort and energy. It also takes discipline. But through it all, our characters are being shaped and strengthened. Even if the reward isn't immediate, the day will come where we will be able to see the fruit of our labor.

What was the last task in which you worked diligently? How did it make you feel when it was done? Are you committed to be diligent in every task even if your efforts go unnoticed? What does your completed work say about who you are?

EXCELLENCE

> By his divine power, God has given us everything we need for living a godly life. We have received all of this by coming to know him, the one who called us to himself by means of his marvelous glory and excellence.
>
> 2 Peter 1:3 NLT

When we think about doing things with excellence, we think of doing them to the best of our ability. To excel is to never stop or settle for less, but always grow and get better.

Excellence is what the Lord desires for us—in our walk with him and our attitudes toward others. He desires us to have a hunger to pursue him and a heart that is willing to be taught by him. When things are done with excellence, whether in music, sports, friendships, studies, or otherwise, we have an understanding that there is always more to learn and achieve. This is the attitude our Father wants us to have regarding our walk with him.

God doesn't want you to settle for "good enough." He wants you to go forward in life, always putting your heart and mind in a position to learn and grow. He doesn't want or expect perfection; he just wants you to *desire* to live with excellence. He can help you with the rest.

What areas, in your walk with the Lord, do you need to adjust in order to walk excellently?

FAITH

Now faith is the assurance of things hoped for,
the conviction of things not seen.
HEBREWS 11:1 NASB

Faith can be challenging at times. When things are going well, it's easy to have faith, but when things are not going as planned, we can be easily shaken. At times, our faith can weaken according to our circumstance.

When a storm arose on the lake where the disciples were, they were filled with fear as their boat rocked back and forth. Jesus began walking toward them on the water. As Peter witnessed this incredible sight, he gained quite a bit of confidence and his faith grew. Peter asked Jesus if he too could walk on the water, and Jesus agreed. Peter got out of the boat and began to walk on the water. But as soon as the waves came, Peter started to sink. His faith was shaken because of his circumstance.

We can be a bit like Peter and lose faith when our circumstances become difficult. It's our faith that determines our outcome. When we place all of our faith in the Lord, he shows up in a huge way.

Are you struggling to have complete faith in a particular area of your life? How can you give it all to God and have full faith that he is working on it?

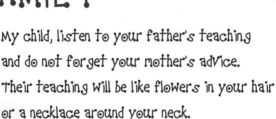

FAMILY

My child, listen to your father's teaching
and do not forget your mother's advice.
Their teaching will be like flowers in your hair
or a necklace around your neck.

PROVERBS 1:8-9 NCV

If someone were to take a group of people all different ages and genders, put them in a house, and say, "Okay you are a family now, so get along, and love each other!" it would be incredibly difficult. It may even be a disaster. Thankfully, that is not the way families are designed. Family is created by God. He designed each of us a certain way and thought very hard about which family we would belong in.

When we are placed in a family, whether through birth or adoption, we are specifically chosen by God to be placed right where we are. Each person within the family is a gift. That's right! Your sister that wears your shirt without asking is a gift. That little brother that totally embarrasses you in front of your friends is a gift too.

It is important to look at each member in our families as a gift from God. Each of us helps the other grow. Maybe that annoying little brother was put there to help us with patience, or the sister who took that shirt is teaches us to be less selfish. God knows where he wants to take us, and training is needed before he sends us out.

Your family is your own personal training ground. It was given in love and it is to be treated with love. So go ahead and enjoy the gifts that have been specifically chosen for you. A gift from God is always one to treasure, respect, and take very good care of.

List each member of your family and write down at least one way they are a gift to you. Thank God for each one and ask him to bless them richly!

FEAR

"Be strong and courageous. Do not fear or be in dread of them, for it is the LORD your God who goes with you.
He will not leave you or forsake you."

DEUTERONOMY 31:6 ESV

Some people are afraid of spiders, others are afraid of the dark. Fears are not uncommon, but we don't usually like talking about our fears. Sometimes we don't share our fears because we are embarrassed or because we feel like we will look weak and silly. But if we bottle up our fears, they have the tendency to grow into huge obstacles that are challenging to overcome.

Fear has a way of strangling our hope and courage. Fear can keep us from living a free and joy-filled life. It can keep us from pursuing our dreams. It can even keep us from making wonderful friendships and experiencing new things. Fears can grip us if we don't give them over to God.

God is our light in the scariest of places. With him by our side, we can face whatever causes us to be afraid. If we lean on him and ask him to help, he will give us a boldness we have never known before. God does not want us to conquer difficulties alone.

What are your fears? Ask God today to help you face them. He is faithful and will free you from whatever is holding you back.

FORGIVENESS

Be gentle and ready to forgive; never hold grudges.
Remember, the Lord forgave you, so you must forgive others.
COLOSSIANS 3:13 TLB

It might temporarily feel good to harbor resentment and bitterness toward someone that has hurt us, but eventually the walls that we build to protect ourselves will only cause us pain. The walls say that the offender doesn't deserve to be forgiven. That somehow, in our own brokenness, we are more deserving of God's love and grace. It is amazing how in our own hurt we can easily forget how we have sinned and desperately need God.

If we ask God for the ability to see our offenders the way he sees them, we gain empathy and a bit of understanding in the midst of our hurt. If we refuse to extend forgiveness, not only are we refusing to love one another the way God wants us to, we are also standing in the way of God's restoration. We are declaring ourselves the judge—a position of authority that no one but God has a right to.

How wonderful that our Judge is one who is fully of mercy and compassion for us! We can trust that he will lovingly make all of the wrongs right. Trusting him completely eliminates our need to withhold forgiveness. Trusting his judgment sets you free from the weight of bitterness and allows God to come in and heal you.

Are you secretly harboring resentment toward someone? God knows how you feel. Ask him to help you forgive, and let him heal your brokenness.

FREEDOM

We have freedom now, because Christ made us free.
So stand strong.

GALATIANS 5:1 NCV

Sin is an ugly thing. We don't feel good after we sin, and yet we still continue to struggle with it. The tough part about sin is that Satan tempts us, roots for us to fail, and then beats us up with shame and guilt. All of this spiritual and emotional chaos makes it hard to receive the freedom offered by God.

You are forgiven. The things you struggle with and the sin that entangles you no longer has power over you. You are set free! When you struggle with sin but have a repentant heart, you are forgiven because of the work Jesus did on the cross. And the cost of forgiveness has already been paid by and through him.

When you sin and then repent, it is finished. God doesn't keep a record of your wrongs. You don't need to rehash, revisit, and recall all the sin. When you entertain your shame, you put spiritual handcuffs on. Your heavenly Father can't wait to make it all right. Receive his forgiveness so he can set you free.

Is there something that you have been beating yourself up about? Take some time to truly let it go and receive the freedom that comes from God's forgiveness.

FRIENDSHIP

Two people are better off than one, for they can help each other succeed. If one person falls, the other can reach out and help. But someone who falls alone is in real trouble.
Ecclesiastes 4:9-10 NLT

God created the concept of friends in the beginning. He first created Adam for himself, and then Eve for Adam. Community is what God desired in the Garden of Eden. He knew that there was much joy to be found in relationship. He knew that we would need companions. Life is lonely without good friends to confide in, to laugh with, cry with, and learn with.

God does not want us to see him as an ominous dictator but as a friend. He longs to talk to us and share in our joy and pain. In the same way, he wants us to have close, healthy friendships with others. When we are purposeful about surrounding ourselves with people who encourage us, challenge us, and love us, we are better because of it.

A true friend is one who loves and supports you through all of life's ups and downs. Friends lovingly tell you when you are making unwise choices, they congratulate you in your achievements, and they always encourage you in your relationship with God. A good friend is one that will pray *with* you and *for* you. Their intention toward you is always good.

When you isolate yourself from the people who love you, you feel alone in the moments you most need a friend. When you hurt, you hurt alone. When you fail, you fail alone. When you celebrate life's triumphs, you celebrate alone. This was never God's intention for you. He wants you to be friends—first with him, and then with others.

What friends are you thankful for today? What could you do to show them how much you appreciate them?

GENTLENESS

A gentle answer deflects anger,
but harsh words make tempers flare.
PROVERBS 15:1 NLT

Most people don't like conflict. Unfortunately, conflict is unavoidable. We all have our own ideas and opinions, so it's not unusual to come up against different viewpoints. We may even find ourselves in disagreement with people we love—like parents, siblings, and best friends.

In the heat of an argument, it is tempting to bite with our words. This is especially true when we feel like we are right, or when we have been wronged and feel justified in our emotions. But fighting doesn't resolve anything; in fact, it only makes the situation worse. Words are powerful: they can be used to love and affirm, or they can be used to hurt. We shouldn't let them flow free without thought.

Our hearts in every conflict should have peace as the end goal. We may not ever come to full agreement, but we can resolve every conflict with gentleness and love. This can be difficult because strong emotions are often involved. If we take deep breaths, and try to step back for some perspective, we can choose to respond in love.

Being gentle means putting yourself in someone else's shoes. It means listening to their feelings. And it means responding softly—with kindness and grace.

How do you normally respond in conflict? Do your words inflict pain and stir up anger? Ask God to help soften your heart and give you a gentle answer.

GRACE

To each one of us grace was given
according to the measure of Christ's gift.
EPHESIANS 4:7 NKJV

Grace can be one of the hardest things to give. We tend to grip it tightly in our hands. We crave justice and can go to great lengths to obtain it. We easily forget the grace God gives us is the same grace he wants us to give others. When we uncurl our fingers and offer grace, we not only free them from hurt, we free ourselves. Grace is such a beautiful gift to give and to receive.

As hard as it can be to give others grace, it can be even harder to give ourselves grace. Sometimes the person in our life that needs the most grace is us. We can be so unkind to ourselves. We berate ourselves for our mistakes and beat ourselves up over our shortcomings. How many times have we called ourselves stupid? Or worthless?

Sometimes we just need to pick ourselves up, dust ourselves off, and give ourselves the okay to try again. We need to not strive for perfection and accept the fact that we are human—just like everyone else around us. Sometimes we will miss the mark. Every mistake is an opportunity to learn. To grow. To change.

Love yourself. See yourself the way God sees you. By giving yourself grace, you will begin to know the love that the Lord has for you. He doesn't hold you to your past or shame you for your shortcomings. He lifts you up, brushes you off, and encourages you to go on. He gives you the grace you need.

How does it look to give yourself a bit of grace today instead of punishing yourself for your mistakes?

GRATITUDE

But I, with shouts of grateful praise, will sacrifice to you.
What I have vowed I will make good. I will say,
"Salvation comes from the Lord."
JONAH 2:9 NIV

When you're young, your parents give you constant reminders to use good manners. One of the most popular phrases in a growing family is, "Say thank you!" There's a reason why parents want to teach the lesson of showing gratitude to others. There is simply nothing better than doing something for someone and knowing that they are thankful for it.

So we thank our friends for a ride, thank our grandma for a birthday gift, and thank someone for having us over for dinner. But when was the last time you thanked God for all that he's done for you? Our Father in heaven wants to know you are thankful for your many blessings too. Even Jonah, sitting in the stinky, dark belly of a giant fish, showed his gratitude to the Lord.

If Jonah can be thankful from the pit of a fish, we can be thankful for all that we have.

Make a list of all that you've been given, and spend some time today thanking the Lord for the blessings he has bestowed upon you.

GUILT

You were taught to put away your former way of life, your old self, corrupt and deluded by its lusts, and to be renewed in the spirit of your minds, and to clothe yourselves with the new self, created according to the likeness of God in true righteousness and holiness.

EPHESIANS 4:22-24 NRSV

Do you ever lie awake at night, thinking of all the ways in which you fell short during the day? Guilt consumes you, making you feel bad about all the poor choices you've made. You toss and turn, unable to sleep because you cannot forgive yourself. It's like a burden you're carrying, weighing you down and making it difficult to breathe.

That's not the life God wants for us! We are full of mistakes, but we don't need to carry that burden on our own. If that were the case, then Jesus would have died for nothing. But he died so that he could shoulder our deadweight for us. We were made new in that moment!

Do you have a burden you're carrying with the shame of guilt? Give it to God. Apologize to those you've wronged, make up for your mistake, release it to the Lord, and move on. He forgives you, so you are free to forgive yourself!

How does it feel to release your burden of guilt to God?

HONESTY

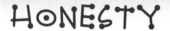

The Lord detests the use of dishonest scales,
but he delights in accurate weights.
PROVERBS 11:1 NLT

Honesty is a great struggle for most of us. We like to bend the truth to get out of a potential consequence, or maybe we don't honestly answer a question because we don't want to offend people, even though we know it's something they should hear.

God teaches us to always be honest. There is freedom in honesty. Lies are a breeding ground for more lies. Bigger lies. The more we lie, the easier it becomes, and suddenly, we find ourselves lying about more serious things.

When we get away with something due to lying, we are often still punished in our hearts because we feel convicted about not telling the truth. Honesty brings things to the light and removes the shackles of lies. Though there may be consequences for telling the truth, it is much better to live a life of freedom from guilt than it is to live for the momentary gain of a lie. That moment never lasts very long.

Is there something you have not been honest about recently?
If so, take a moment to confess it to God and then make it right.
Ask him to help you see the value of being honest.

HONOR

Be devoted to one another in love.
Honor one another above yourselves.
ROMANS 12:10 NIV

Your school or neighborhood is probably filled with many kids that come from different walks of life. Some kids have a lot of money, some do not; some are considered "cool" and others not so much. There are kids that have talents that make them popular, while others have important talents that are hardly recognized. Have you noticed who most people choose to be friends with?

When we think about Jesus and his friends, we remember that he befriended the underprivileged, the tax collectors, and the not-so-popular. When these individuals got to know Jesus as a trusted friend, they felt honored and loved for who they were. He honored others above himself. Because of this, their lives were forever changed.

It is easy to honor, love, and be friends with those that are like us, but it is Christ-like to look for those who may need a friend and make them feel loved and respected by honoring them above yourself.

Is there someone in your school or neighborhood that you feel needs to be shown more honor, love, and respect? How might you honor them above yourself?

HOPE

May the God of hope fill you with all joy and peace as you trust in him, so that you may overflow with hope by the power of the Holy Spirit.

ROMANS 15:13 NIV

Hope is expecting an ideal outcome against all odds. People can put their hope in many different things, but the return of that hope won't be very successful if it's not rooted in Christ.

God asks us to put our hope in him. When the ground is being shaken beneath us and things seem out of our control, we make our requests to the Lord and then believe with full confidence that he has heard.

Placing our hope in the Lord begins with giving him the desires of our heart and then truly trusting him with those desires. He honors the hope we have in him and he knows how weak our hope can be. Sometimes it can be scary to place great hope in him for fear of being disappointed. This is where we need to trust and accept that our loving Father knows what is best for us. If we hope for something that is not to our benefit, then he won't grant our request—for our good!

Hope big and trust in God. He always wants what's best for you—what will bring you closer to him. He wants to hear your requests and lavish you with his love. What are some hopes that you would like to tell God about?

HUMILITY

When pride comes, then comes disgrace,
but with humility comes wisdom.
PROVERBS 11:2 NIV

Our talents are a gift from God. We all have different talents and we should take good care of them. We can use them to bless others and bring glory to God. Often when people have been gifted with a talent, they like to receive the credit and bring attention to themselves. This is the absolute opposite of what God asks of us.

It is important that we view our talents not as our own, but as a tool to bring honor and glory to God. It can be tempting to be proud and boastful, but the more we walk in humility with our talents, the more we allow God to reach others through our talents.

Humility comes when you are confident in God's opinion of you, so you don't use your talent to seek attention from others. It comes when you choose to use your talent to honor God simply because he is worthy of it. It comes when you recognize that you have no talent without God.

Are there ways in which you can act more humbly in your God-given talents? Thank him for the gift of your talents and make a list of how you can start using them to bless others!

IDENTITY

To all who believed him and accepted him,
he gave the right to become children of God.
JOHN 1:12 NLT

Based on the sheer volume of quizzes to be found online, it is easy to determine that we are a culture desperate to know who we are. We try so hard to be identified by our personalities, our hobbies, and our interests. Are we intellectuals? Writers? Artists? Musicians? Engineers? We spend so much time on a crusade to discover who we are, even letting others—sometimes people we don't know—speak into our lives and define our identity.

Truly, you are so many things. But above all, you are a child of God.

Knowing who you are is the anchor for getting you through difficult and confusing situations in life. You belong to God. You have a place in his family and an identity that is highly valued.

Are you worried? Don't be. You are a child of God.

Are you afraid? Don't be. You are a child of God.

Do you feel lost and alone? You aren't. You are a child of God.

Let the truth pierce your heart. You are the daughter he loves so much, he will go to the ends of the earth for you. Like a loving father watches over his daughter, God watches over you.

Are you searching for who you are? Do you desperately want to discover your identity? Make a list of who God says you are. Start with these: you are the daughter of a King, you are loved, you are wanted, you are valued, you belong, you are known. Wrap yourself in these truths today.

INFLUENCE

No one lights a lamp and then puts it under a basket. Instead, a lamp is placed on a stand, where it gives light to everyone in the house. In the same way, let your good deeds shine out for all to see, so that everyone will praise your heavenly Father.
MATTHEW 5:15-16 NLT

When our lives are captured by God and completely changed, we can't help but want access to a microphone to declare his goodness to the world. But we don't always have to be standing up in front of a class, shouting God's word for everyone to hear in order to be an influence.

Our influence can be even more impacting and valuable by simply following God. If we allow him to direct our lives, people can see firsthand how life-changing God is. Our influence will be our unshakeable joy in trials. It will be the way we defer to the weak and lonely with a compassion that only comes from knowing God's compassion in our own lives. It will be in the way we include the unloved and outcast. It will be the way we give our lunch money to the one who needs it. It will be in the way we visit the sick and care for the widows. Be encouraged that God is using you, even when you don't have a microphone in your hand.

Light. Joy. Peace. These are things that people crave. Our words do not carry as much weight or influence as our actions do. People want sustenance; they crave authenticity. Our influence can be in the simple, everyday way we handle ourselves.

The platform we have is a strong but subtle one. We can either influence people to live for God or for themselves.

People are watching the way you handle yourself in stressful situations. Are you gentle with others? Are you compassionate? Are you generous with your time and money? Are you quick to humble yourself and ask for forgiveness if you have hurt someone? As God's child, you are a light in a very dark and sad world. Don't be afraid to shine for him.

INSPIRATION

Generation after generation
Will declare more of your greatness,
And discover more of your glory.
Your magnificent splendor
And the miracles of your majesty
Are my constant meditation.
Your awe-inspiring acts of power have everyone talking!
And I'm telling people everywhere about your excellent greatness!
PSALM 145:4-6 TPT

With technology and social media right at our fingertips, it's difficult to be inspired by the things God intended for inspiration. Minute by minute, our heads are down trying to connect with others. But what about the magnificent beauty that's also at our fingertips?

God made us to be creative and he wants to inspire our creativity. That's why he gave us towering mountains, hand painted skies, starry nights, rippling rivers, amazing wildlife, and the changing of seasons. What he made was well thought out and it was all made with us in mind.

God knows we need his beauty not just to inspire us, but also to feed our spirits in a powerful way. He wants to meet with us in the quiet moments and teach us more about himself. It's in these sweet places that he wants to tell us he loves us.

Gifts from God are all around you. Lift up your head and allow yourself to be inspired. As you go about each day, look for God's beauty. Write down what aspects of God's creation inspire you the most. Then thank him for them!

INTEGRITY

People with integrity walk safely,
but those who follow crooked paths will slip and fall.
PROVERBS 10:9 NLT

Do you live confidently and carefree? When you choose to live with integrity, you will. We have nothing to fear when we live in the truth, but when we choose dishonesty, we spend our days in constant fear of being found out.

It's a lot of work to hide the real story from others. Stories have to be kept straight, details have to be remembered, and it's a battle to think of the lies we've told. In the end, we are always discovered.

God doesn't want us stumbling about our days unsure of our footing and watching out for every step we take. He wants us to live free of the cares and burdens we carry when we keep secrets and live in the shadows. He wants us on the secure path of truth.

Pray that you will remain on the path of honesty, honor, and virtue. Put one foot in front of the other, secure in the knowledge that you will not stumble. Stay off the crooked path, and keep your eyes on the straight and narrow one ahead of you!

What are you often tempted to lie about? Choose integrity. It's a lot easier in the long run.

JOY

Splendor and majesty are before him;
strength and joy are in his dwelling place.

1 Chronicles 16:27 NIV

There is a significant difference between feeling joy and feeling happy. *Joy* goes beyond the basics and infuses *happy* with some extra oomph. And it can only truly come through Christ our Lord. He is the source of our great pleasure!

You see, happiness is a temporary feeling. Joy stays with us. Happiness flees in the midst of tough times, but joy is there regardless of our circumstance. It's a fruit of the Spirit, produced only by God's work in us. It's a gift from him! When we are aware of his grace and favor, then joy can truly come.

Experiencing the Lord's joy doesn't mean you'll never feel sadness again. Hard times come to everyone regardless of our maturity in faith. Pray that you will feel great pleasure in your life no matter what comes your way. Put your trust in him. He loves you, and wants to share all of his gifts with you.

Take some time to ask God for the spirit of joy today!

JUSTICE

"For I, the Lᴏʀᴅ, love justice;
I hate robbery and wrongdoing.
In my faithfulness I will reward my people
and make an everlasting covenant with them."
Isaiah 61:8 NIV

It's not fair! How did she get away with that! We have all thought that before when someone hurts us or is dishonest about something and doesn't get caught. Sometimes things are unfair, and it's hard to ignore them. We want justice, and we want it now!

There is a lot of injustice in this world, and it can be frustrating, sad, and confusing to think about. There is hope. God teaches us in his Word that he is just. This means he stands for justice. All who have greatly wronged others will either be led to repentance or will receive the appropriate consequence in the end. He sees and knows it all. He is quick to love and slow to anger, but those who hurt his children and do not repent will be punished.

Sometimes we have a hard time waiting for justice. We don't want to wish it on others; however, it is comforting to know that if we do not see immediate consequences for wrongdoing, we can rest assured that our loving and protective God saw it, and he will make it right.

What are some ways you can make things right with people you have wronged or people who have wronged you? Can you change your heart toward them and pray for God's mercy?

LEADERSHIP

"I am the good shepherd.
The good shepherd lays down his life for the sheep."
JOHN 10:11 NIV

What do you look for in a leader? If we are to bring others into a relationship with Christ, we are all called to become leaders ourselves. One of the best examples we could ever ask for in leadership was Jesus himself. And he called himself a good shepherd.

There was good reason for this. Though a shepherd, at the time, was not a job that many aspired to, it called for special skills. A shepherd had to guide his flock of sheep without scaring them into submission. Sheep are known to make poor choices when operating under fear.

Shepherds needed to nourish, comfort, lead, correct, and protect their sheep. And most importantly, a good shepherd would encourage those in their care to follow his example and stay with him.

Are you a leader for Christ's kingdom? Are you encouraging others to follow your example, comforting them in times of need and correcting them gently when the situation calls for it?

Spend some time today writing down all the ways you can display leadership in your life, modeling yourself after the good shepherd—Jesus Christ.

LIFE

Therefore, I urge you, brothers and sisters, in view of God's mercy, to offer your bodies as a living sacrifice, holy and pleasing to God—this is your true and proper worship.
ROMANS 12:1 NIV

Sacrifice. That's not a very comfortable word is it? We don't think of it as being easy or as the popular choice. What does it mean to be a living sacrifice?

As God's followers and children, we should live in a way that honors and blesses him. It is so difficult to live that kind of life with all of the temptations of this world and everything at our fingertips. In fact, we can't live a holy and pleasing life *and* give into the temptations of this world. We fall into the trap of doing what we want: buying too much stuff, dressing to fit in, gossiping about others, being ungrateful—these are just a few things we need to watch out for.

If you practice each week to work on an area in your life that you feel hasn't blessed the Lord, then you will feel something change, and you'll receive the confidence that only your Heavenly Father can give. By living this way, you are sacrificing your desires and truly worshiping him. *That* is pleasing to God.

What sacrifices can you make that would please God?
How hard will it be to let go of those things?
Remember, sacrifice isn't supposed to be easy.

LONELINESS

A man of many companions may come to ruin,
but there is a friend who sticks closer than a brother.
PROVERBS 18:24 ESV

Most of us are not strangers to feeling lonely from time to time.
We know what it feels like to be sad, without a friend to call on for
comfort and company. We can feel lonely in our grief. We can feel
lonely in our accomplishments. We can even feel lonely in a room
surrounded by tons of people. Imagine that: having all the friends we
could ever want or need and still feeling lonely.

Feeling like no one cares or understands us is a difficult place to
be. Sometimes all we wish for is someone to be there. Someone to
listen to our needs and genuinely care.

Do you know that you are never truly alone? God is with you
always. Even in times when you feel the most alone, he is there. He
promises never to leave or forsake you. When you feel loneliness
pressing in, before you even call out to him, he is already there.
There is so much comfort in knowing that in all our journeys we do
not travel alone.

Do you feel lonely today? Reach out to him and ask for his
presence to comfort you. He cares deeply for you.
How does it feel to know that God is always with you?

LOVE

Know therefore that the Lᴏʀᴅ your God is God; he is the
faithful God, keeping his covenant of love to a thousand
generations of those who love him and keep his commandments.
Dᴇᴜᴛᴇʀᴏɴᴏᴍʏ 7:9 ɴɪᴠ

Because we are human, it can be really hard to think of God's
love in any other way but how we know it with other people. And
with other people, it can often feel like there are strings attached. If
you let someone down, if you don't live up to their expectations, you
may see them start to slip away or reject you.

Though we may find this hard to believe, rejection is *never* the
case with the Lord's love. It is unconditional. There is nothing you can
do to make him turn away from you. He designed you before you
were ever a wisp of your mother's imagination. You are one of his
chosen people, and he is faithful to those he loves!

Do you believe that God loves you unconditionally? Or do you
somehow feel that there are strings attached? If so, close your eyes
and picture a giant pair of scissors snipping right through all of those
strings. They don't exist in your relationship with God.

Thank God today that he loves you through the good
and the bad.

MODESTY

I want women to be modest in their appearance. They should wear decent and appropriate clothing and not draw attention to themselves by the way they fix their hair or by wearing gold or pearls or expensive clothes.
1 TIMOTHY 2:9 NLT

Leggings, short shorts, tops that fall off one shoulder, and shirts that show a little stomach are all considered fashionable today. It is so common for young ladies to visually give themselves away.

So many young women forget that the inside is the most important! What do our hearts gain when others are tempted to look our way because of what we're wearing? What do our hearts gain when we receive flattering comments that we are prettier and more fashionable than others? Our hearts gain *nothing*.

Insecurity and a desire to please others can cause us to dress or act inappropriately. Being modest takes courage and confidence. Stay true to yourself and know that what God has placed in you is enough. Be the girl who knows and loves who she is. Fashion is fun, and it can be used to express who you are! But your body is a temple—a house in which the Holy Spirit lives, so dress it in a way that honors the Lord.

How do you feel about being modest? Take a minute and ask God to show you if you are dressing to gain attention from others. Are there items in your closet that need to be eliminated because they are not honoring your body or the Holy Spirit that dwells within you?

OBEDIENCE

Blessed are all who fear the LORD,
who walk in obedience to him.

PSALM 128:1 NIV

Why is obedience to God so important? Simply put, our obedience is a demonstration of our love for him. Though good works don't give us eternal salvation (only a relationship with Jesus can do that), if we truly love God, then we have a desire to follow him and live a life of good deeds. We will want to follow the example set by Christ and live our lives modeled after him.

There are times when everything in us wants to rebel against what we're told to do—whether it's to clean our rooms, stay away from bad influences, or turn homework in on time. But a life in Christ is one that is transformed.

It may not be easy, but it is possible to begin to desire to walk on the path God sets for us. If you feel like rebelling today, set that feeling down before the Lord. Ask him to give you a heart change, so that you *want* to walk in obedience.

Make a list of the many ways Jesus obeyed his Father when he was on the earth. Thank God for giving you an amazing model of obedience and for transforming your life.

PATIENCE

Live a life worthy of the Lord and please him in every way:
bearing fruit in every good work, growing in the knowledge
of God, being strengthened with all power according to his
glorious might so that you may have great endurance and
patience, and giving joyful thanks to the Father, who has
qualified you to share in the inheritance of his holy people in
the kingdom of light.
Colossians 1:10-12 NIV

One of the hardest things to do is to wait. The countdown to
something fun can feel like it takes a million years. The time spent
waiting for big news may feel like an eternity.

Paul knew this difficulty even back in his day, thousands of years
ago. He implored the people of Colossia to be patient, and to feel a
spirit of joy even while they waited for what they wanted. But that joy
can come only from the Lord. It's much too hard to find it on our own!

Are you waiting patiently for something? Pray that you can
experience joy through the waiting. Ask the Lord to fill your heart
with true happiness and patience until the day you are hoping for
finally comes.

Write down some of the things you are waiting for now,
and believe that your answers will come one day!

PEACE

"Submit to God and be at peace with him;
in this way prosperity will come to you."
Job 22:21

Did you know that God designed our bodies to require rest? It seems like a luxury to have rest in this day and age, and the ability to truly enjoy it becomes difficult. Our minds begin to think about the things that we need to get done, or perhaps we get distracted by other people and things clamoring for our attention.

Like a car that needs to be filled with gas and have the occasional oil change to operate correctly, our body, mind, and spirit need peace and rest to operate well. The peace that God wants to give us is a supernatural peace. It's a peace that feeds us in all areas of our lives and restores our souls. All that is required of us is to recognize that we *need* his peace, and then to take the time to slow down and meet with him.

Maybe it's an hour on the couch, or a quick prayer and a deep breath in the hallway at school. Either way, the key is to seek him first and not as a last resort after total burnout. Our bodies will start shutting down if we are not aware of our need for rest. We have to stop plowing forward with so little gas in our tanks, and go to God. He is abundant in peace and faithful to give it when we ask.

Is there a particular area in your life where you need God's peace? Take a moment to talk with him about it and then *rest* in him.

PEER PRESSURE

Whoever walks with the wise becomes wise,
but the companion of fools will suffer harm.
PROVERBS 13:20 ESV

History shows us that we tend to follow the masses. It is natural to want to fit in, to be included, to feel part of something bigger than ourselves. But we need to be careful who we are trying to fit in with.

We need to guard our hearts and listen to that tiny voice of reason deep within us. When we don't, we can find ourselves in situations that are over our heads. God gave us wisdom to make good decisions. That tiny voice that seems so relentless and strong? That is the Holy Spirit given to us by God to help us choose wisely.

Often the hardest part of resisting peer pressure is the precise moment we need to say no. When we gather the courage to stand up for our values and morals, a feeling of peace will rush in. That peace is worth every moment of feeling uncomfortable. We may be temporarily mocked for walking away, but the choices we make today could have a huge impact on our future. It might seem fun and harmless to join the crowd in the moment, but the damage done to our futures could be devastating.

God wants to help you resist peer pressure. With him you are stronger, braver, and wiser than you think. When you choose to walk with God, you won't stumble because he is with you every step of the way. Let the Holy Spirit guide and help you. Listen to his voice and recognize his presence.

Do you feel pressured to be someone you are not? Pressured to ignore your beliefs in order to be accepted? Do you find yourself behaving in certain ways to be part of the crowd? How can you set your heart on walking with God? Ask him to help you stand against peer pressure and fill you with his peace.

PERSEVERANCE

We are surrounded by a great cloud of people whose lives tell us what faith means. So let us run the race that is before us and never give up. We should remove from our lives anything that would get in the way and the sin that so easily holds us back. Let us look only to Jesus, the one who began our faith and who makes it perfect. He suffered death on the cross. But he accepted the shame as if it were nothing because of the joy that God put before him. And now he is sitting at the right side of God's throne.

Hebrews 12:1-2 NCV

If you are an athlete, then you know what it means to persevere. Pushing yourself past your wall, breaking down what you thought were your limits, and hanging on to the end are all a part of an athlete's way of life.

Our lives as Christians are like a marathon. There is the world's greatest prize waiting for us if we can push through and endure until the end. When we cross the finish line, we get to run into the arms of Jesus. Hardship will come, but we can get through it if we just keep our eyes on that prize.

Are your eyes on the prize of life with the Lord? As you spend time with God today, ask him for his assistance in helping you through the tough times. Pray for the ability to persevere. The prize waiting at the end is worth it!

What do you look forward to most about the final prize?

PROTECTION

"Because he loves me," says the L○○○, "I will rescue him;
I will protect him, for he acknowledges my name.
He will call on me, and I will answer him;
I will be with him in trouble,
I will deliver him and honor him.
With long life I will satisfy him
and show him my salvation."

Psalm 91:14-16 NIV

At some point in your life, there will come a time that you will look around and suddenly realize that you've found yourself in an uncomfortable situation. You may not even be sure why it is that you feel so icky, but you know that you don't feel good about what's happening. In these times, you can call a parent, or you can call a trusted friend. But before you call anyone else, you should first call on God for protection.

God wants to protect you and keep you safe. The Bible tells us several times that he is our protector. And while this doesn't mean that harm will never befall you, it does mean that he will deliver you. The way he brings you through it might look different than you expected it to.

Pray for protection over your life today. Ask God for his help when tricky situations arise, and he will deliver you.

In the past, have you prayed for protection when you've found yourself in uncomfortable situations? Make a plan to do that now, so when the time comes, you will be ready!

PURITY

Teach me more about you;
How you work and how you move,
So that I can walk onward in your truth,
Until everything within me brings honor to your name.
PSALM 86:11 TPT

With today's constant access to media, it is a huge challenge to keep our thoughts and motives pure. Everywhere we look we are bombarded with images that are sexual or inappropriate in nature. Many TV shows, movies, and song lyrics have underlining sexual themes.

Sex sells; purity is not so popular. Fighting against that grain is a tiring battle. Media teaches that it's okay to act and dress inappropriately, and that it is perfectly acceptable to engage in sexual relationships outside of marriage.

Purity is a matter of the heart. When we aren't careful to guard our hearts, we open the door to pain, confusion, and hurt. It is impossible to erase what we have already seen. Nor can we easily forget what we've heard. We need to be so careful with what material we expose ourselves to. Everything can have a positive or negative impact on our hearts and minds.

Because God loves you so much, he wants you to be protected from the evils of this world, even if those evils are carefully covered up in humorous story lines and interesting plots. Keeping your heart pure may require you to avert your eyes, re-think some of your relationships, set up boundaries, and say no to some social media outlets. It may seem extreme to go to such lengths, but by taking precautions, you become protected from a world of hurt.

By making purity a priority, you are not only honoring God, you are honoring the beautiful person God created you to be. You are worth being safe-guarded. Your mind, your heart, and your body all hold value. Do you truly believe this to be true in how you live? How can you make purity a priority starting today?

PURPOSE

Whether, then, you eat or drink or whatever you do, do all to the glory of God.

1 Corinthians 10:31 NASB

Too often we measure our worth based on what we do or on what our status is. We love to label ourselves because it gives us a sense of self-worth: *I am an honor student. I am a star athlete. I am a ballet dancer.* We all have this need to know what drives us: to know why we wake up in the morning. So we cling to labels as if our lives depend on them. If our current situation does not meet up to our expectations, we feel worthless and insignificant. A life without meaning is a sad one without hope.

The good news is that we all have purpose. Every single one of us has purpose that cannot be measured: young or old, teacher or student, mother or daughter, doctor or janitor. If we live for God, we are exactly where God wants us to be, doing exactly what he wants us to do. We don't have to go on an extravagant crusade to find our purpose. We don't have to have straight A's or don ballet slippers to have meaning.

Our purpose is to love God, abide in him, know him, and serve him. We just have to embrace it. It is simplicity at its finest. Too often we complicate the subject and go wandering in search of our life's purpose—we already have an opportunity to live purposefully every single day!

Do you feel like you are constantly trying to figure out what your life's purpose is? Stop searching and know that you have purpose right where you are. Your life is significant and valuable. How can you embrace your God-given purpose today?

REDEMPTION

In him we have redemption through his blood, the forgiveness of sins, in accordance with the riches of God's grace.
EPHESIANS 1:7 NIV

Have you ever seen anyone at a restaurant insist on paying for a bill twice? Not likely. Nobody in their right mind would pay for a bill that was already paid for in full, would they? It wouldn't make any sense. Yet we all fall into this terrible habit of reminding ourselves of our past mistakes and sins. We allow ourselves to be entrapped in what once was and forget that we are already redeemed. Our sins were already paid for. We are free and clear. Sin free. Debt free.

It doesn't matter who we were or what we did in the past. In God's love for us, in his mercy and grace, not only has he forgiven you and me, but he has redeemed us from a life of despair. He has taken what was once lost and broken, and transformed it into something beautiful.

Your history is wiped clean. You are completely free from condemnation, guilt, and punishment. He took all that upon himself so that you could live a new life. That is how much he loves you! In him, you are a new creation. You are no longer tied to who you once were.

He has redeemed you. What a beautiful, undeserved gift it is to walk away from imprisonment and embrace freedom. Accept God's gift of grace—the washing and undoing of sins. Unshackle yourself from the past, and lift your face to the one true King who has set you free.

Do you keep forgetting that you are redeemed? Write down the truth of his redemptive work in your life and let it seep into the very core of who you are. You are redeemed.

RELIABILITY

Do not swear, either by heaven or by earth or by any
other oath, but let your "yes" be yes and your "no" be no,
so that you may not fall under condemnation.
JAMES 5:12 ESV

Promises are so easy to make, but can be so hard to keep. Anyone can make a promise, but it takes a reliable, trustworthy person to follow through. Sometimes, we can be yes people when we really shouldn't.

We might say yes because we don't want to disappoint our loved ones. Or we say yes because we are unrealistic with time constraints and try to shove too many things into a short time span. Or we say yes because it is too hard to pass up an exciting opportunity. Sometimes we say yes when we should really say no.

Our culture is not one that allows a lot of down time. We fill up our schedules with studying, activities, and work, not allowing any breathing room or time to rest. We don't give ourselves permission to say no when we should. So we commit, and then we over commit.

The problem with over-committing is that, inevitably, we will burn out. When we fail to deliver, we really fail to be trustworthy. Our intentions may be for the best, but if we make a habit of not following through with our commitments, people around us will begin to see us as unreliable and untrustworthy. It can be hard to change others' opinions of us when we constantly let them down and disappoint them.

When you aren't reliable, it reflects on your character. It is always better to think carefully about a new venture or opportunity before you commit to it. Measure if you can be depended on. If you have to say no this time, maybe the next time you will be able to say yes. There will always be another opportunity.

How do you think you are seen by the people around you? Do you have a reputation of being reliable? How can you show others they can trust you to do what you say you will do?

RESPECT

Respect everyone, and love your Christian brothers and sisters. Fear God, and respect the king.
1 Peter 2:17 NLT

We were given a very powerful tool when God chose to give us the gift of speech. It can be used to bless, encourage, and even worship the Lord. Or it can be used as a weapon to destroy and cause great pain.

We all have spoken and heard words being used both ways. It feels much better to give and receive loving communication than it does to give and receive destructive communication. When we think about how Jesus used his words, we know that he used them to bless and speak love. We also know that if there was a conflict, he used truth and wisdom to confront those who were being foolish.

Often we use cutting remarks to point out faults, instead of speaking truth with respect. We need to learn how to truly love others with our words—even when that involves honest evaluation.

Whenever you are tempted to lash out with your words, take a breath and think about how Jesus responded to those opposing him. Make your words match his example so they will truly count.

Take a moment to write down a strategy for speaking respectfully the next time you are tempted to blurt out something hurtful.

REWARD

In all the work you are doing, work the best you can. Work as if you were doing it for the Lord, not for people. Remember that you will receive your reward from the Lord, which he promised to his people. You are serving the Lord Christ.

COLOSSIANS 3:23-24 NCV

It can feel pretty good when we do something above-and-beyond and then receive recognition through praise or a reward. It's ok that it feels good. If someone recognizes us for doing a good job, great! However, there are some people that can't wait to tell others about their achievements or acts of service so they can receive instant gratification and praise. This type of strategy is not what brings worth in the eyes of the Lord.

It is God's heart for you to do things not for the reward and praise here on earth, but to keep the good things that you do between you and him. When you choose to do this, you are building up treasure in heaven. If you show goodness to others and then choose to keep it quiet, you will be greatly rewarded. Don't worry. Your Father in heaven always sees. He doesn't miss a thing. Someday your reward will be of great worth!

Are there areas in your life where you have been seeking an instant reward? Take a moment to ask God to help you in these areas and to give you the grace to keep it between the two of you.

ROYALTY

Listen, daughter, and pay careful attention:
Forget your people and your father's house.
Let the king be enthralled by your beauty;
honor him, for he is your lord.
PSALM 45:10-11 NIV

Beautiful princess adorned with grace, you were created for greatness. You are *royalty*. Your Creator, the King of kings, is your heavenly Father.

Heavenly Father is not just a name that we use loosely as another way to describe God. He is *actually* your Father, and he is *actually* the King of all kings. The royal standard in countries that have kings and queens is that daughters born of the king are born into royalty because of who their father is. Your Father is the King, and he adores you.

We need to fully understand what it means to be God's princess. We have a very special calling. Representing what a young woman should be, in the eyes of the Lord, is very important. The music we listen to, the clothes we wear, and the shows we watch all reflect on our position as princess. If we take pride in being royalty and want to represent our Father's kingdom well, we are more likely make decisions that will bring him honor.

As a princess, with what areas of your life do you best honor your Father, the King? Are there areas that you need to refine? Rest in the knowledge that your Father loves you just because you are his princess.

SELF-CONTROL

Think clearly and exercise self-control. Look forward to the gracious salvation that will come to you when Jesus Christ is revealed to the world.

1 PETER 1:13 NLT

Every day we face situations where we need to exercise self-control: in our attitudes toward others, especially when we disagree with them; with our friends when faced with peer pressure; with social media and maintaining healthy boundaries and time limits; with school assignments or commitments in making sure we try our best.

Sometimes the pressure or expectation to have self-control can be overwhelming—especially when we are struggling with habits that are proving difficult to break free from. We might feel like we are at the mercy of our temptation.

The wonderful news is that we don't have to be controlled by our own desires, whims, or strongholds. We are not weak; in fact, God has made us strong. There is no need to become frustrated with our sin. Instead, we can hold our heads high and defeat whatever habit enslaves us or temptation that entices us because God has given us self-control. There is hope to be free from old patterns. We *can* be patient with our family, we *can* resist peer pressure. We *can* develop healthy habits and boundaries with social media. God's power lives within us!

We don't have to let our sin patterns control our lives. We can take charge, make changes, and break bad habits.

In what areas of your life do you need to exercise more self-control? Don't forget that self-control isn't something you have to muster up; it is already in you! Take hold of it, and take back control today.

SELF-ESTEEM

Listen, my dearest darling,
You are so beautiful—
You are beauty itself to me!
SONG OF SONGS 4:7 TPT

Do you ever hear voices in your head that tell you you're not good enough? Do you need others' approval and opinions to give you confidence in a particular area? There is good news: you are enough! God made you just the way he wants you. Those voices in your head that say you're not good enough are lies.

You can do anything God calls you to. When the voice of discouragement comes, silence it. When you find yourself desiring approval, shift your thinking to seek God for confidence. What God thinks of you matters the most.

The more you practice dwelling on the truth, the more you will see how valuable you are in your Maker's eyes. Allow him to define you and be proud of who that is. Who God has created you to be is much better than anyone you could even *try* to become on your own!

In which areas of life do you feel most insecure?
Write out a prayer, asking God to help you become
more confident in those areas.

SERVICE

Your love must be real. Hate what is evil, and hold on to what
is good.... Do not be lazy but work hard, serving the Lord
with all your heart. Be joyful because you have hope.
Be patient when trouble comes, and pray at all times.
Share with God's people who need help.

ROMANS 12:9, 11-13 NCV

How many times a day do we see our hands but fail to recognize their potential, their power, their ability? Our hands can be used to bless many people around us. They can wipe away tears. They can work. They can comfort. They can *serve*.

We often think of serving others as a job for those in ministry: pastors serve, missionaries serve, humanitarians serve. But serving is something we can all do.

There are many practical ways to serve those around us. We could give our time to a lonely friend. We could help a fellow student with their homework. We could buy a meal for someone in need. We could spend an afternoon cleaning our elderly neighbor's home or visit a friend who is in the hospital. These simple examples require a sacrifice of time.

Think back to the last time you were served. Maybe someone finished a task that you were dreading or unknowingly provided for a great need. In an act of service, we not only receive a tangible gift, we also catch a glimpse of God's love for us. When we serve others, we are being used by God to show his love.

God made us to love each other and to give ourselves to each other. It might mean helping with jobs that don't seem rewarding or pleasant. But there is both joy and eternal blessing to be found in serving.

How can you serve someone today? Ask God to show you who is in need of your time or resources, and then go and love them.

STRENGTH

Do you not know?
Have you not heard?
The LORD is the everlasting God,
the Creator of the ends of the earth.
He will not grow tired or weary,
and his understanding no one can fathom.
He gives strength to the weary
and increases the power of the weak.
Even youths grow tired and weary,
and young men stumble and fall;
but those who hope in the LORD
will renew their strength.
They will soar on wings like eagles;
they will run and not grow weary,
they will walk and not be faint.

ISAIAH 40:28-31 NIV

No matter how puny your muscles may seem to you, you are stronger than you know. You can do anything you set your mind to. And you'll do it because God gives you a supernatural strength to power through and endure.

God never wearies. He never gets too tired to make it through the worst the world can throw at you. Put your hope in him, and he will give you strength beyond your wildest imagination.

Others around you may stumble and fall, but not you! Ask God to give you the tenacity to make it through your toughest of times. He wants to run with you until the very end.

In what areas do you feel weak right now? Ask God for strength in each one. He loves it when you admit your need for him. It's when he gets to show off his strength the most!

STRESS

Therefore do not worry about tomorrow,
for tomorrow will worry about its own things.
Sufficient for the day is its own trouble.

MATTHEW 6:34 NKJV

Many young people today are overwhelmed and overbooked. Life is fast and it doesn't want to slow down for anyone. There are multiple assignments to complete, tests to study for, instruments and sports to practice, chores to do, and friends you need to keep up with. And if that's not enough, you may feel it all needs to be done with excellence.

Time out! When you are feeling stress creep into your life, it is important to get back to where God wants you to be. He wants you right next to him. He wants to gently walk with you and teach you how to look at stressors differently. All you can do is try your best and that is enough. Did you get that? *Trying your best* is enough. Nobody expects you to have super powers.

Often we put an unnecessary pressure on ourselves because we only see things through our own eyes. When we begin to spend more time with Jesus and ask him to help us see things as he sees them, we can begin to accept that trying our best is enough.

What areas of your life are most stressful right now? Ask God for the confidence to stand through the stress, knowing that doing your best is all that matters.

TEMPTATION

No temptation has overtaken you that is not common to man.
God is faithful, and he will not let you be tempted beyond your
ability, but with the temptation he will also provide the way of
escape, that you may be able to endure it.

1 Corinthians 10:13 ESV

Wouldn't life be so much easier without temptation? Temptation
has this sneaky way of pressing in on every angle of our lives. It
surrounds us. It can be relentless, and it is always unwelcome. Often
it feels like we can't look left or right without being presented with it.
The misconception is that if we are tempted, then we must be weak
in our faith. This is not true. No one is immune to temptation—even
Jesus was tempted. The struggle was as real for him as it is for us.

We don't have to give into our temptation because in every
moment of every day we are given choices. God's grace lies in those
choices. We can bend a knee to our temptress and give up, or we
can take up the shield of faith and fight.

When our temptation becomes too much for us to bear alone,
we can go to the church, loved ones, or trusted family members
and friends to help us. Shedding light on dark areas is a great way
of escape. Those who really love us won't judge us; they will offer
grace, compassion, and understanding. We shouldn't feel like we
have to battle temptation alone. God gives us others to battle
alongside us—we just have to be bold enough to ask them for help.

What temptation are you fighting? Don't attempt to battle
it alone. Share your *struggle* with a trusted friend who will
pray with you and for you. How do you feel about sharing your
temptation with *someone*? Bring light into the dark areas and you
will find renewed hope!

TRUST

Trust in the Lord with all your heart,
And lean not on your own understanding;
In all your ways acknowledge Him,
And He shall direct your paths.
PROVERBS 3:5-6 NKJV

There can be seasons where things don't seem to work out in your favor and life seems harder than normal. It could be issues related to relationships, school, sports, or even family dynamics. When things are tough in these areas, it tends to greatly affect our feelings, our mindset, and even our trust in God. We might feel like we're in the desert all alone.

The good news is that God knows just where we are. We are not lost. Many times when we are walking through difficult situations, the Lord has allowed us to experience those difficulties to test what is in our hearts. He is refining and maturing us. Though it may feel like he is far away, he's actually close by, molding and shaping us like a potter does with clay.

The next time you find yourself in one of these seasons, don't stop trusting God! Go to him immediately and ask him what he wants to teach you. When you make yourself vulnerable and willing to learn, he will reveal the things he is working on, and assure you that there is purpose to your season in the desert. Trust in him and he will carry you through!

Are you struggling to trust God in this season?
What do you think he might be trying to teach you?
Ask him! And then be willing to learn.

TRUTH

Lead me by your truth and teach me,
for you are the God who saves me.
All day long I put my hope in you.
PSALM 25:5 NLT

When we think of truth, we often think of confessing something we've done that was not wise. But truth is also shown in the encouraging words we say to others and the life we live as representatives of God.

Living a life for truth means to live in a way that stands for truth in all circumstances. It can be difficult to speak truth when there is a chance we may offend someone, be met with awkward silence, or stand with the minority.

You may find yourself in a situation where you feel the need to stand for what is right, but you're unsure you can find the courage to do so. Likely the Holy Spirit is nudging you to speak out in truth. If you listen to that nudge and obey it, you open a door for God to touch others.

God loves when you stand for him, especially during difficult times. He sees what you do and say during those times, and he knows how hard it is for you. It blesses him beyond measure to see your boldness. As you continue to walk in truth, he will use you in great ways, and he will prepare a beautiful place for you in heaven!

In what areas do you feel you need to be living
a more truth-focused life?

VALUE

"For where your treasure is, there your heart will be also."
MATTHEW 6:21 NIV

Clothing, shoes, popularity, and name brands are some pretty common things valued by younger girls. It's pretty difficult not to value these things yourself. But what has *true* value?

God wants us to focus on valuing things that are of him—things like love, generosity, righteousness, and honesty. These things bring lasting value because they add to the kingdom of heaven. Clothing and popularity are temporary; they can be taken away or destroyed in a single day. They are not life giving and really have no value.

If you happen to be popular, or can afford those name-brand boots, that's fine, but the moment you find yourself being motivated by, and becoming focused on, those things, you have given it too much value. You can't place equal value on shoes and righteousness; it just doesn't work that way.

God is not impressed by name brands. He is, however, very impressed by the love he sees in your heart, the honest words you speak, and the generosity you display. Be aware of what you find valuable because that is what your heart will spend the most time going after.

What do you think is valuable in life? Is there something on which you have been placing too much value? Reevaluate it. See what it is actually worth, and adjust it accordingly in your priority list.

WHOLENESS

He heals the wounds of every shattered heart.
PSALM 147:3 TPT

Sometimes when we look closely at ourselves, all we see is a broken and shattered remnant of what we once were. Sin, tragedy, rejection, or heartbreak can leave us feeling terrible. We wonder how we can pick up the pieces and be made whole again.

In our brokenness, it's easy to feel hopeless. We try so many methods to fill the void. We may look to relationships, things, or drugs to fix us. They can make us feel better temporarily, but eventually we realize that despite all our efforts, we still feel broken and incomplete.

Who could possibly love and care for such a broken and tattered person? Jesus. He loves you. *All of you.*

God is faithful. He doesn't leave us alone in our brokenness, instead, he meets us in our ugliness, takes our broken pieces, and tenderly puts us back together again. Why? Because he loves us too much to leave us in the state we are in. He wants us to experience healing and restoration.

In him we find wholeness that the best doctor or medicine can't even provide. He is the only one that can heal our pain completely. His love is so deep it can even remove scars.

God can heal all those inner parts that you feel are beyond repair. You can trust him in your brokenness. Tell him today just how much you need him.

WISDOM

If you need wisdom, ask our generous God, and he will give it to you. He will not rebuke you for asking.

JAMES 1:5 NLT

Have you ever made a decision because most people around you thought it was truly a good idea, but it somehow didn't feel right to you? On the flip side, have you ever made a decision about something that made others think you were crazy, but deep down you knew it was the right thing to do? These are examples of two different kinds of wisdom. The first decision was made with worldly wisdom; the second with Godly wisdom.

The Bible teaches us that God's wisdom looks foolish to those who don't have a relationship with him. It also says the things that seem wise to the world are often foolish in the eyes of God. It seems a little confusing. The good news is that we don't have to have it all figured out. God gives us the Holy Spirit to help guide us.

That voice that you hear deep inside is often the Holy Spirit guiding you closer to the plans that God has for you. The more time you spend with your heavenly Father, the louder the voice of the Holy Spirit becomes within you. And the more you choose to walk in that Godly wisdom, the more Godly wisdom you will receive. Soon you will feel confident and certain when he speaks because you will recognize his voice.

Don't be intimidated by what others think and say. Trust in the wisdom of God. Everything he does is for your good. He cannot wait to share more of his heart with you. Take the leap and walk in God's wisdom. You will not be disappointed!

Ask the Lord to show you where you need more of his wisdom. How do you feel he is leading you to walk in his wisdom?

WORRY

Can all your worries add a single moment to your life?
MATTHEW 6:27 NLT

It's easy to worry about the future. How am I going to do on my test? Are we going to win that big game? What will she say when I confront her? Will I get that job? These are a few examples that can send our minds racing.

What is the point of worry? Has worry ever helped anyone feel better? Has it ever solved the problem? No. Each day has enough problems of its own. It is better to take each day one step at a time and let God lead us through it. The things that are for tomorrow will still be there tomorrow, and that's where they should stay for now. Then, when the time comes, we can ask God for help.

Everything that you walk through with God is not going to be easy, but worry does not have to be part of it. If you seek God during those times, you can have confidence that he has heard you, and he will work out his good and perfect will.

We can often rehash things and stir up all kinds of new worry. Don't go there. Let God take care of it, and allow yourself to let it go. Everything is not always going to land in our favor, and everyone isn't always going to be thrilled with us. We can try our best, but the real work belongs to God.

Where are your most common areas of worry, and how can you let God carry you through them? Take rest and comfort in knowing that your Father is *for* you. He is more than enough.

WORTH

You formed my innermost being,
Shaping my delicate "inside"
And my intricate "outside,"
And wove them all together in my mother's womb.
I thank you, God, for making me so mysteriously complex!
Everything you do is marvelously breathtaking.
It simply amazes me to think about it!
How thoroughly you know me, Lord!
Psalm 139:13-14 TPT

God doesn't make mistakes. Take a deep breath, and then read that again. God doesn't make mistakes. He just doesn't. When we read in the Book of Psalms that he created us from the very beginning of our existence, from fingertips to toes, we know that he did it with purpose, and that he did it flawlessly.

It's so easy to let the things of this world dictate how we feel about ourselves. If we don't have enough of such and such, or our circle of friends feels too small, or if we don't have the latest item, it feels like we are not quite worthy enough.

But you were created to be a masterpiece! You are lovely and you are loved simply because that is how he made you. Because you belong to the Lord, you are enough.

God doesn't make mistakes.
You are worthy because he made you worthy.
Repeat this to yourself today: "I am enough because I am his."
Now write it down, and begin to believe it!